FAMOUS PEOPLE
FAMOUS LIVES

Biographies of famous people to
support the curriculum.

KT-555-637

John Lennon

by Harriet Castor

Illustrations by Richard Morgan

W

FRANKLIN WATTS

LONDON•SYDNEY

First published in 2000
by Franklin Watts
This edition 2002

Franklin Watts
96 Leonard Street
London EC2A 4XD

Franklin Watts Australia
56 O'Riordan Street
Alexandria, Sydney
NSW 2015

ISBN 0 7496 4350 1

A CIP catalogue record for this book is
available from the British Library

Dewey Decimal Classification
Number: 780.92

10 9 8 7 6 5 4 3 2

Series Editor: Sarah Ridley
Designer: Jason Anscomb

Printed in Hong Kong

John Lennon

In 1940, during World War Two, a baby boy was born in Liverpool in the middle of a bombing raid. His name was John Winston Lennon – 'Winston' after the Prime Minister, Winston Churchill.

John's father, Fred, was away at sea. Julia, John's mother, hardly ever saw Fred and soon Fred and Julia split up. When Julia met another man, she decided it would be better if John went to live with one of her sisters, Mimi.

Aunt Mimi loved John dearly
but she was strict with him too.

At school John often got into trouble. He was the leader of a gang of friends and he was always fighting, or joking around.

Although he was clever, he wasn't interested in lessons. The only subject he liked was Art.

John failed all his school exams. By now though, he had found something that did interest him: a new style of music called 'rock and roll'.

One singer in particular, Elvis Presley, was inspiring hundreds of teenagers to set up their own bands. John decided to set one up, too.

The band was called The
Quarrymen, after John's school,
Quarry Bank High. John had
never learnt music, but Julia
bought him a cheap guitar.
She could play the banjo, and
she taught him some chords.

The Quarrymen played at parties and church fêtes. One day, a friend brought someone along from another school.

His name was Paul McCartney and he could play the guitar.

John asked Paul to join the band
and they became great friends.
Aunt Mimi didn't approve of the
band at all, so they practised at
Paul's house.

Soon a friend of Paul's joined too,
a boy called George Harrison.

When John was seventeen, his mother was killed in a road accident. John was very sad.

By now John was at Art College, but he spent all his time writing songs with Paul and playing with the band. Another art student, Stuart Sutcliffe, had joined them. Stuart had a bass guitar and was trying to learn to play it.

At this time, the group changed their name every time they played! Then John had an idea...

There was a famous group called The Crickets and this made John think of beetles. He changed the spelling so it was like 'beat music', which was what people called the new music the band played.

Soon The Beatles began to play in some of Liverpool's clubs. One club owner had connections with clubs in Hamburg in Germany and The Beatles went to play there. But they had no drummer, so they asked another friend, Pete Best, to join the band.

In order to go to Hamburg, John had to leave Art College.

Mimi thought it was a big mistake.

In Hamburg, the club where The Beatles played was very rough and there were lots of fights. They had to sleep in a cinema and sometimes played for eight hours a night.

But they loved it – they learnt
to play really loudly and jump
about on the stage to keep the
crowd entertained.

When they returned to Liverpool, The Beatles were a better band and they were different, too. 'Rock and roll' music was also becoming more popular and was even shown on TV.

Soon The Beatles had lots of Liverpool fans. They played a great deal, which was hard work, but fun. They went back to Hamburg, too. Stuart decided to stay there and he married one of their German friends.

People began asking for Beatles' records in a shop run by a man called Brian Epstein. Brian hadn't heard of The Beatles, so he went to a club they played in called The Cavern.

Brian decided he wanted to be The Beatles' manager, even though he didn't know anything about managing groups.

The Beatles liked the look of him, so they said yes.

Brian set about organising the band. He gave them schedules to follow and told them not to eat or smoke on stage. He told them to wear smarter clothes, too.

Although they were famous in Hamburg and Liverpool, no one else had heard of The Beatles. Brian tried to get them concerts in new places, but without much luck.

25

The key to success was making records. Brian set up auditions with record companies in London.

At first the companies said no, but eventually in 1962 one record producer, George Martin, agreed to take The Beatles on.

John, Paul and George asked Brian to sack Pete Best, their drummer. They wanted another drummer called Ringo Starr to join the group. Pete Best had lots of fans in Liverpool and they were furious.

That summer, John's girlfriend Cynthia found out that she was pregnant. She and John got married, but they tried to keep it a secret from all of the jealous Beatles fans.

Cynthia had a baby boy.
They decided to call him Julian
after John's mother, Julia.

Meanwhile, The Beatles' first
single came out – 'Love Me Do'. It
reached Number 17 in the charts.

Their second single 'Please Please Me' was the first of many Beatles Number One hits. This was the success that they had always dreamed of.

By the end of 1963 they were so popular, people had started talking about 'Beatlemania'. Crowds of screaming fans followed them everywhere they went.

Soon, they were famous all around the world, and very rich too.

Being so popular had its problems. John, Paul, George and Ringo couldn't live like the rest of us. They couldn't walk down the street, or sit in a café. Sometimes they even had to put on disguises to escape the crowds of fans.

Though he loved being successful, John sometimes made mistakes and he hoped he wouldn't be famous for ever.

The Beatles spent nearly all their time touring. Then, in 1966, they decided to stop. The fans screamed so much at their concerts, they couldn't hear themselves play. They thought they were getting worse as musicians, not better.

They all wanted to do other things as well as being part of The Beatles. John acted in a film. Later, they all went to India to study Eastern religion.

In 1967, their manager, Brian, took too many sleeping pills and died. The Beatles were very sad. They had lost one of their closest friends. They were worried too – Brian had looked after all their money and no one knew what to do without him.

They set up a company called Apple, hoping to help other musicians, artists and writers. But Apple didn't do very well.

The Beatles' records were still an enormous success. As ever, John and Paul wrote most of the songs, but their music was always changing and developing.

George was influenced by Indian music and taught himself to play the sitar.

They all contributed ideas and often worked for hours in the recording studio until they had got their songs just right.

The other Beatles were the most important people in John's life – even as important as Cynthia and Julian. But that changed when, one day, John met a Japanese artist called Yoko Ono and fell in love with her.

John and Cynthia got divorced
and he and Yoko Ono began
to go everywhere together.
She even sat beside him in the
recording studio.

Meanwhile, The Beatles had started to quarrel with one another. They decided to split up but they still managed to have fun recording their last ever album, 'Abbey Road'.

John went on to make many
more records. He and Yoko Ono
also campaigned for peace. In
1975 they had a son, Sean. John
gave up recording for several
years to spend time with him.

In 1980, John started recording again. He was living with Yoko and Sean in New York. One night, on his way home from the recording studio, a fan shot him dead in the street.

The other Beatles were devastated by the news. Despite all their quarrels, they loved each other very much. Thousands of John's fans around the world were devastated, too.

Further facts

Paul, George and Ringo

Like John, Paul, George and Ringo all went on to make their own records after The Beatles split up. Paul set up a successful group called Wings and made some solo records, too. George became a successful film producer. Ringo acted in several films and also did the voice-over for the TV series 'Thomas the Tank Engine'.

Lennon and McCartney

The Beatles and their music are still very popular. Their records sell in large numbers all around the world. John Lennon and Paul McCartney are one of the most famous and successful song-writing partnerships ever.

Memorabilia

Many people collect Beatles memorabilia – anything and everything to do with the group. When, for example, musical instruments, photographs, scribbled notes or autographs come up for sale at auction houses, they are sold for very large amounts of money. The house in Liverpool in which Paul grew up has been taken over by the National Trust so that it can be visited by the public.

47

Some important dates in John Lennon's lifetime

1940 John Winston Lennon is born in Liverpool, son of Julia and Fred.

1956 John forms a band called The Quarrymen with school friends.

1956 John meets Paul McCartney and asks him to join the band.

1957 John becomes a student at Art College.

1958 John's mother is killed in an accident.

1959 The group change their name to the The Beatles.

1960 The Beatles' first trip to Hamburg.

1961 Brian Epstein becomes manager for The Beatles.

1962 John marries Cynthia Powell.

1962 The Beatles' first British single, 'Love Me Do', is released.

1963 John and Cynthia's son, Julian, is born.

1967 Brian Epstein dies.

1969 John marries Yoko Ono in Gibraltar.

1975 John and Yoko's son, Sean, is born.

1980 John is shot dead in New York.